D1284760

HOW TO SURVIVE ON A DESERT ISLAND
OPERATION ROBINSON!

Text by Denis Tribaudeau

Illustrations by Karine Maincent

Schiffer Publishing Ltd.

4880 Lower Valley Road • Atglen, PA 19310

CONTENTS

ARRIVING ON THE ISLAND 7

WHAT DO WE DO ONCE WE ARE WASHED UP ON A DESERT ISLAND? 8

❭ Where to begin? 9
❭ Three essential things 10
❭ Conserve your strength 11

THE FIRE 13

A FIRE IS ESSENTIAL FOR SURVIVAL 14

❭ Choose the best technique 15
❭ Prepare the ground and material 15
❭ Lighting the fire 15
❭ Putting out the fire 17

THE SHELTER 19

BUILDING A SHELTER 20

❭ Choose the ideal site 21
❭ Choose the correct building technique 21
❭ Building 22

DRINKING WATER 25

HOW TO FIND DRINKING WATER OR HOW TO MAKE WATER FIT TO DRINK 26

❭ Can we drink sea water? 27
❭ Finding drinking water on your island 27
❭ Make a machine to collect drinking water 28
❭ Boil water to make it drinkable 29

KNOTS 31

❭ Make coconut rope 32
❭ Half-hitch knot 32
❭ Reef knot 32
❭ Bowline knot 33
❭ Highwayman's hitch knot 33

FISHING AND TRAPS   35

CATCH FISH AND MAKE TRAPS   36

❱ Catch and trap fish, mollusks, and shellfish   37
❱ Catch and trap crabs and insects   38
❱ Making a "fishery"   39

EDIBLE PLANTS AND FRUIT   41

SAFETY WHEN EATING PLANTS AND FRUIT   42

❱ Recognize edible plants easily   43

SIGNAL YOUR PRESENCE   47

HOW TO LET PEOPLE KNOW YOU ARE THERE   48

❱ Make distress signs that can be seen from a plane   49
❱ Being seen from a ship passing a long way away   50

READ THE SKY   53

STARS AND CLOUDS   54

❱ Understanding the sun's movements   55
❱ Using the stars to find the north   56
❱ Other remarkable constellations   57
❱ Recognize different clouds to predict the weather   57

PREVENTION AND TREATMENT   59

PROTECTING YOURSELF AND APPLYING FIRST AID   60

❱ Protect your skin from the sun   61
❱ Scrapes and cuts   61
❱ Blisters on your feet   62
❱ Insect and jellyfish stings   62

THE LONE CASTAWAY

Have you ever dreamed of being a great adventurer, lost on a desert island like Robinson Crusoe? This could become a game!

The weather is good; the sun is hot and high in the sky. With your friends, imagine that you have just been washed up on the beach of a deserted tropical island, along with a few objects saved from a sinking ship. You'll have to be crafty enough to survive and as clever as a brave explorer. You'll have to invent everything, make everything, and build everything, as well as fishing, treating wounds, eating, and making a fire with whatever is at hand!

If you know where to look, nature will give you everything you need. With a little imagination, you can transform any material to create an extraordinary story full of surprises and discoveries!

It won't always be easy, but with a bit of dexterity and a moral strong enough to face any danger, nothing is impossible.

So close your eyes, imagine your island, and let's head for adventures!

ARRIVING ON THE ISLAND

WHAT DO WE DO ONCE WE ARE WASHED UP ON A DESERT ISLAND?

Any castaway will tell that there's nothing funny about being washed up on a deserted beach. It's a very stressful moment because it's not what anyone would wish for and often happens after being in a shipwreck or plane crash.

Even the famous Alexander Selkirk, who inspired Daniel Defoe to invent the story of Robinson Crusoe, didn't become a lone castaway on purpose.

However, nowadays people can volunteer to try the experience, under controlled conditions, of surviving on a desert island.

You can become a voluntary castaway too!

STEP 1

❯ Where to begin?

If you were shipwrecked, you would have to think quickly about finding a place to alleviate your stress and get organized. First of all, you shouldn't stay on the sand, which would probably be very hot; you should find a place in the shade and put on a hat and a T-shirt (or use sun block) to protect your head and skin from the sun. If you are wet, you should get dry as soon as possible, because water—even warm tropical water—will make you cold twenty-five times faster than the air! Once this is done, take several deep breaths to calm yourself so you can think straight.

9

STEP 2

〉 Three essential things

Here is a list of the things you might want to do to survive. Sort the actions into order of priority by putting numbers from 1 to 13 in the boxes (1 is the most important, 13 the least important).

What are your top three priorities?

☐ **Make a shelter**

☐ **Sleep awhile to recover your strength**

☐ **Exercise to get rid of your stress**

☐ **Find drinking water**

☐ **Find batteries**

☐ **Make a bow and arrows**

☐ **Build a latrine**

☐ **Light a fire**

☐ **Go for a swim to cool down**

☐ **Search for food**

☐ **Make a raft**

☐ **Fish**

☐ **Put up a distress signal to help someone find you**

If your three answers were to make a shelter, light a fire, and find drinking water, bravo! Go to the top of the class! It's also important to find food or signal your presence, but these tasks will come later. To reach your first goals, empty out your pockets and any bags you have been able to save. You'll probably find several useful objects or tools to help you. Then walk along the beach to find odds and ends the sea has washed up on the shore between the rocks. You'll be sure to find a lot of stuff. Take time to gather as much as you can.

STEP 3

❱ Conserve your strength

Knowing how to save your strength is a basic survival rule. Take time to find shady paths and go around obstacles to avoid tiring yourself out unnecessarily. Don't run, and avoid carrying heavy objects.

THAT LITTLE EXTRA

If there are several of you on the island, get yourselves organized to be as efficient as possible. So that everyone has a chance to offer ideas without being interrupted, choose an object (a shell, stone, or stick) to use as a mic. This is called the "baton," and only the person with the baton in his or her hand is allowed to speak, while the others listen. Once the person has finished putting forward his idea, he or she passes the baton to the next person wishing to speak.

DID YOU KNOW?

Robinson Crusoe never existed. He was invented by the writer Daniel Defoe, who was inspired by the survival story of Alexander Selkirk. On the other hand, that story is true: Alexander Selkirk lived alone on an island for four years!

SAFETY FIRST!

✗ While thinking about something or while resting, stay in the shade to avoid getting too hot or sunburned.

✗ Be careful while walking on rocks when looking for useful items, as rocks are often slippery and dangerous. Don't go barefoot!

✗ If you are wet, dry yourself properly to avoid catching cold.

THE FIRE

A FIRE IS ESSENTIAL FOR SURVIVAL

A fire is the most important thing to have because it is essential for survival. It protects you from big and small insects, gives you light, allows you to cook food and heat water, creates a signal for rescuers, keeps you warm, and finally, it reminds you that you are a human being, as no animal on Earth can light a fire.

But be careful: fire is dangerous and destructive!

To learn how to light one, you must be with an adult. It's very hard to get a flame, so patience and caution are key!

STEP 1

❯ Choose the best technique

Look around and decide how you are going to go about making your fire. What is the weather like? Is it warm and sunny, or is it cloudy and perhaps about to rain? There are two ways of lighting a fire: by using the sun, or by rubbing two sticks together if the sky is overcast. Remember to ask an adult for advice.

STEP 2

❯ Prepare the ground and the material

Once you have chosen your technique, get everything ready. In the forest and on the beach you will find dry material. You need dry grass, small twigs, small pieces of deadwood, and bigger pieces of wood. There is always lots of wood on a desert island beach. Remember to have a bottle of water close by that you can use to put the fire out if necessary.

Choose a dry, level spot to make your embers and flame; it will be a lot easier on level ground. Dig a hole in which to make your fire; this will allow you to put out the fire by covering it with dirt when you leave. Cut up the pieces of wood.

DID YOU KNOW?

It is extremely important to be careful with fire. Every year, because of carelessness and fires not properly put out or lit in the wrong place, giant fires destroy entire forests, killing lots of animals and rare plants and burning down houses. In France alone, an area equivalent to twice the size of Paris is burned every year. A lot of people are seriously harmed by smoke from wildfires. Huge clouds of ash particles pollute the air we breathe and contribute to global warming.

15

STEP 3

❯ Lighting the fire

LIGHTING THE FIRE ON YOUR OWN USING A MAGNIFYING GLASS AND THE SUN

This is the easiest way to get your fire going, and you can do it on your own.

Aboard your ship you found a magnifying glass or other object that has a magnifying effect, such as a camera lens or eyeglasses. Set up your things in the sun, remembering to put on your hat. Make a ball of dried grass and hold the magnifying glass between the ball and the sun. You'll see the little point of light when the sun's rays heat the grass, and smoke will start rising almost at once. To get a flame, blow gently on the grass.

LIGHTING A FIRE BY FRICTION WITHOUT THE SUN

Materials

- **Small wooden board**
- **Wooden stick (a drill) with the end sharpened into a point**
- **Object to protect your hand, such as a shell**
- **Bow made from a branch and a piece of string**

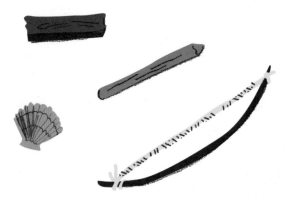

Ask an adult to help you prepare your board by making the beginning of a hole near the edge with a knife. Wind the sharpened stick (drill) into the bowstring. Place the shell between the stick and your hand to protect it. Press the tip of the drill hard into the small hole in the board, using your feet or knees to pin the board flat on the ground. Move the bow back and forth from left to right to make the drill turn very fast. The drill will make the hole in the board larger. When the hole gets close to the edge, ask an adult to cut a notch in the wood, as you can see in the picture.

fire seems to be out, bury it with the earth or sand you scraped out when you made your hole. Place a small wooden cross over the hole to show future visitors to your desert island that the fire is out.

Make a small "nest" of dry grass or straw and keep it close by. Place a large leaf under the notch. Place the drill in the notch and use the bow to turn it very fast. You will see black sawdust forming, and soon smoke will appear. When the notch is filled with black sawdust, stop turning the drill and carefully remove the board. Put the hot sawdust into the nest of dried grass and blow gently on it to get the flame going.

STEP 4

》 Putting out the fire

As fire is very dangerous, you must be careful to put it out before you leave. Pour lots of seawater over it. You'll see a lot of steam rising; be careful not to burn yourself by standing over it. Once the

A bit of history

This technique is very old. It was used by American Indians and prehistoric Ethiopians. Even today, some people use this technique to light fires.

SAFETY FIRST!

- ✗ Never light a fire unless an adult is present.
- ✗ Clear the ground around your fire pit to avoid setting the forest alight.
- ✗ Use lots of water to make sure the fire is put out properly.

THE SHELTER

BUILDING A SHELTER

Why build a shelter?

All creatures on Earth, from the smallest to the largest, need a place where they can rest and sleep safely. Therefore it is important that you build your shelter properly.

You can nap in a shelter and even spend the night there. It protects you from the wind and rain and keeps you safe from danger once night has fallen. You can store fragile things in a shelter and use it as a dry place in which to recover your strength.

STEP 1

❯ Choose the ideal site

Quite often, nature shows you the ideal spot for your shelter, so look around to see what it offers. Don't set up camp on the beach. Farther inland you'll probably find a small cave, a big hollow tree trunk, a leaning tree, or a bush with lots of branches that naturally form the framework for your shelter. All you'll need to do is make a roof with pieces of wood. You'll find several places where deadwood has piled up, and you'll be able to make your shelter with this material that is easy to gather.

If you build your shelter on the beach, you risk getting washed out when the tide comes in and losing your provisions! Look at the band of seaweed left by the last high tide; that's the highest point the water will reach at high tide, so install your camp a lot higher than this line. The ideal place for a shelter is hard, flat, and shady, overlooking the beach. The trees will protect you from the damp sea air and the sun. They will keep you cool and block the sound of the waves, which can get on your nerves after a while, as long as your shelter faces inland.

STEP 2

❯ Choose the correct building technique

You've found your spot, but there are no caves or trees to help you start your shelter. So make it simple and efficient! Use everything you can find on the beach. Unfortunately for nature, but luckily for you, the world's beaches are gathering places for all sorts of rubbish that washes ashore: boards, fishing nets, rope, bags, cloth, tarpaulin. Take all this back to your campsite.

THAT LITTLE EXTRA

Use only deadwood that has fallen from the trees. Not only will this preserve living trees, it's easier to pick up fallen branches than trying to cut them down with a knife or saw!

STEP 3

❱ Building

A SHELTER WITH ONE OR TWO PARTS

This is the easiest shelter to make! Even without rope you can fix a large piece of wood—a beam—between two branches where they form a "Y" ①. Then lean branches against the main beam as shown in the picture ②. Finally, cover the branches with leaves or with a tarp ③. If you are lucky to find large leaves, you can cover the frame as you would tile a roof, starting from the bottom.

A PYGMY HUT

To make this hut, gather a lot of long, supple branches. Start by tracing a circle in the dirt. Then plant the branches into the ground every fifteen inches or so (about the length of a stride). Bend the branches toward the center and tie them together to form an igloo-like structure. Then make it stronger by tying on horizontal branches, which will be useful for fastening on a cover made of leaves, grass, or a large tarp.

A TEEPEE

For this, you will need at least seven or eight long, thick poles and a tarpaulin or old bed sheet. Create a bundle with your poles and tie them together at the top with rope. Find the center at the top of your tarpaulin and make a hole in it. Slip a long piece of rope through the hole; this will be used to tie the tarpaulin to the central pole. With the help of at least one grownup, raise the poles and set them upright in a circle, making sure that two poles are spaced far enough apart to allow entry. Finally, spread your tarpaulin around the frame and fasten it to the two entry poles.

23

SAFETY FIRST!

✗ Get a grownup to check that your shelter is solid and that nothing is likely to fall on you.

✗ Make sure the branches are solid by banging them on the ground (they shouldn't break).

✗ Be careful when gathering leaves and branches; sometimes insects or snakes hide under them and you don't want to get bitten.

✗ Don't build your shelter under a coconut palm – falling coconuts can cause serious accidents.

24

DRINKING WATER

HOW TO FIND DRINKING WATER OR HOW TO MAKE WATER FIT TO DRINK

Having drinking water in your camp is vital, especially in the height of summer, to avoid getting dehydrated!

If you don't have enough with you, you'll have to find more on your island, because without water, you won't last long: even the greatest adventurers can't survive more than four days without water!

❭ Can we drink seawater?

On your island you are surrounded by millions of gallons of water, which might tempt you to drink it! But be careful, seawater isn't drinkable because it's far too salty and causes serious health problems. It will make you throw up. However, you can dilute a little seawater in your drinking water, even if it doesn't taste nice! If you respect the proportions of one volume of seawater to seven volumes of drinking water, you can extend your water supply without getting sick.

❭ Finding drinking water on your island

To find water, you'll have to head inland. Like any explorer, you will carefully follow paths in the forest made by animals. They need to drink too; perhaps their paths will lead you to a river or a waterfall! Once you have found fresh water, follow it to its source, where it is likely to be less polluted.

If an expedition isn't possible, look at the plants around you and search in the base of their large leaves, in the holes in fallen trees, or inside bamboo; there is probably a little fresh water to drink. Coconuts are full of liquid you can drink. Ask a grownup to help you make holes in the hard shell.

If it starts to rain, it will be a great help! Rainwater can be drunk in small amounts. Set out your containers and make a collector with a poncho, jacket, or tarp (as in the picture below). You'll find that the water tastes good, and it is cold.

THAT LITTLE EXTRA

- To get the milk out of a coconut, you must pierce the shell without breaking it. To do this, drive a metal or wooden spike through two of the three "eyes" in the shell (a screwdriver is best). Pour the milk into a glass or suck it out of one of the two holes you have made.

- To drink a small amount of water from the base of a leaf or inside of a tree trunk, find a rush stalk or tube and turn it into a straw for sucking up the water!

❯ Make a machine to collect drinking water

If you aren't lucky enough to find water and your island is completely arid, all is not lost! You can make a "sun distiller."

First, find a spot in the sun and dig a big hole. Put a mug in the center of the hole and surround it with green leaves and damp grass. Seal the hole with a large piece of transparent plastic. Don't forget to place a small stone on the plastic directly over the mug; this will guide the drops of condensation to the mug. Wait a few hours for enough water to drip into the mug before drinking it.

❯ Boil water to make it drinkable

This is the best solution to make sure your water is drinkable, but be careful not to spill the boiling water on yourself, or you'll get a bad burn. Always ask the help of a grownup before undertaking this task. Fill your pot with water and hang it over your fire; let it boil at least ten minutes to kill the germs that would make you sick.

A little history

Having drinking water arrive by the tap in our homes is normal and natural. However, even today, more than two billion people on the Earth don't have access to safe, clean drinking water.

SAFETY FIRST!

✗ To be certain to drink water that won't poison you, carry water-purifying tablets with you; they are really efficient. This is medication, but it's easy to use. Ask your parents to seek your family doctor's advice.

✗ If you have any doubts about the water quality, be careful: if it smells bad or has a brackish taste, if it is muddy or green or brown, or if it is salty, don't drink it!

✗ Just because water is fresh and clear doesn't mean it is drinkable! **If you have any doubts, boil it and ask a grownup for advice.**

KNOTS

❭ Make coconut rope

If you don't have a rope on your desert island, coconut palms can come to the rescue! You'll need to be patient and rather strong to make a coconut rope, but it's worth the effort! For good results you'll need:

- **A coconut**
- **A large, flat stone**
- **A log or a mallet**

First, search for old coconuts that have spent a lot of time in the sea. You'll find them between rocks where the high tide has left them.
Try to remove the hard inner shell and keep the husks. Place the husks on the flat stone and beat them with your piece of wood or mallet. You'll be able to reuse the fibers that are attached to the husks.
Lay the fibers in the sun to dry them, which might take a few hours.
Finally, with four or five fibers you can make a solid tress. You can join the fibers together to make your rope longer.

❭ Half-hitch knot

This is the easiest knot to make! It is perfect for tying your tarpaulin to a branch, for example.

Pass your rope around your support (a ring, branch, or pole). Bring the short end of the rope behind the longer part (called the Standing Line) ① and ②, pass the end through the loop you have just made, pull it tight, and repeat the first two steps ③ and ④. If you think your knot might not be solid enough, add extra loops.

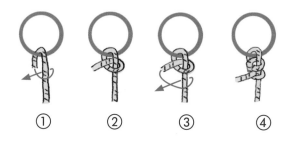

①   ②   ③   ④

❭ Reef knot

You can use this knot to join several lengths of short rope together to make a longer one!

Using two ropes, place the right-hand rope over the other. Wrap the right-hand rope under the other ①. Bring the right-hand rope back over the other ②. Bring the end of the right-hand rope over the other. Pass the right-hand rope under the other rope ③. Pull the bottom two pieces of rope ④ to tighten the knot ⑤.

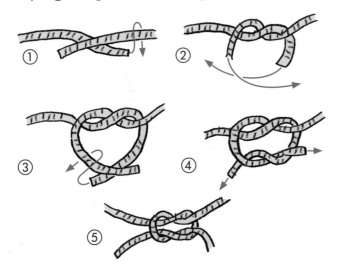

❱ Bowline knot

This is a classic knot! It forms a solid loop and is easy to undo.

Make a little loop by crossing the rope over itself ①. Pass the short end of the rope up through the loop ②. Pass the end under the Standing Line. Pass the end back over the Standing Line ③. Pass the end back into the small loop and pull it tight ④!

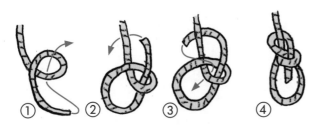

❱ Highwayman's hitch knot

This is a solid, efficient knot for tying canvas to a pole, for example. Above all, it can be undone very quickly. All you have to do is to pull on one end for the knot to undo, and you can escape . . . like a highwayman!

Double the rope to make a loop and place it behind your support—a tree trunk, for example. Make a second loop in the Standing Line and pass it through the first loop ①. Pull a little on the shorter end of the rope to hold the second loop in place ② and ③. Take the working end and make a third loop ④. Pass the third loop through the second and pull on the Standing Line to tighten the knot ⑤ and ⑥.

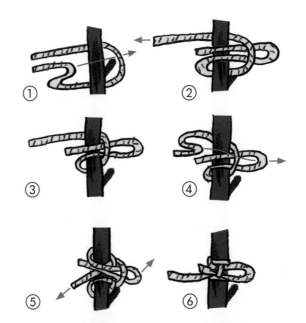

FISHING AND TRAPS

CATCH FISH AND MAKE TRAPS

This is the most complicated survival task!

It will take all your concentration and skill to make your hunting strategies work.

You will quickly discover that making traps is less tiring than running after a big animal with a lance, however. Also, small fish, insects, crabs, and shellfish are easier to find and will give you all the energy you need.

❯ Catch and trap fish, mollusks, and shellfish

• Collecting shellfish

This is the first step in finding food easily! But be careful not to slip and fall while walking on wet, seaweed-covered rocks. Once you have collected enough shellfish, rinse them in fresh water if possible and cook them thoroughly to kill any bacteria that might make you sick.

• Catching fish with a harpoon

To make a harpoon, you'll need a long, straight pole (about your own height). You split it in two along a length of about eight inches and tie a cord at the base of the split. Then place a small piece of wood between the two halves to keep them apart; now cut some notches on the outside of each half to keep the fish from sliding off the end of your harpoon. Then lie in wait over a pool of water for a fish to show up. When it does, harpoon it with a quick downward movement.

• Make a basket for crabs

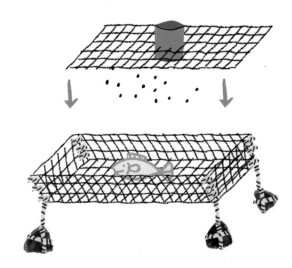

You might find some interesting rubbish on the beach, such as wire netting, a bit of tube, and string. Tie the wire netting with the string to form a basket. Make a hole in the middle of the top of the basket and insert the piece of tube in it. Now put the basket in a rock pool. If you can find a rotting fish, use it as bait inside the basket. All you have to do now is to wait.

37

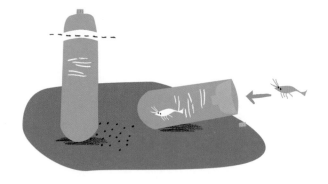

• Make a trap for fish and prawns

Cut the top off a plastic bottle and put the neck inside the bottle. Put your trap in a rock pool and watch the small fish and prawns swim into the bottle. The more appetizing your bait (bread or rotten fish), the more your trap will fill up.

DID YOU KNOW?

Today a lot of people in the world only trap fish for food. Sadly, some of them use drift nets several miles long that destroy biodiversity by indiscriminately trapping all sorts of fish, turtles, sharks, and dolphins. Others practice dynamite fishing that kills everything! These methods are now illegal.

❱ Catch and trap crabs and insects

• Make a trap for crabs

Some crabs live in water all the time and others wait on the beach for high tide. They are often very quick and not easy to catch. Here's a trick to help you catch them easily. Look through the rubbish you have found on the beach and see if you have something that looks like a bowl (a coconut half will do). Now copy the illustration below and set it up on hard ground. As soon as the crab touches the bait, the bowl will fall and imprison it.

• Catch insects

If you have a small fishing net, go out and hunt grasshoppers. They are all edible!

❭ Making a "fishery"

Look around your island to see if there is a place where the rocks form a half-circle or a horseshoe. It could even be a very large half-circle! Now make sure that this place is completely covered by the sea at high tide and easy to reach at low tide. Wait for the tide to go out and use stones to change the half-circle into a closed circle, a little like a swimming pool. When the tide comes back in, the water will cover your pool. When the tide goes out again, you might be lucky to find several fish trapped in your pool. All you have to do now is catch them!

A little history

Huge "fisheries" still exist on Oléron Island, France. The islanders made these traps to imprison very big fish. At each low tide, the fishermen gathered the trapped fish. They also checked the giant "horseshoe" to make sure it hadn't been damaged by the sea, as it was made of stones piled on top of each other. Storms and the current could destroy it in a few hours. The biggest fisheries had a circumference of about half a mile.

SAFETY FIRST!

✗ Don't run on rocks, because you could slip and fall on oysters or other sharp surfaces and hurt yourself badly.
✗ Thoroughly cook all animals, shellfish, and insects you catch. The heat from your fire will kill all the bacteria that could make you sick.
✗ Don't eat brightly colored animals or insects: it's often a sign that they aren't edible.

EDIBLE PLANTS AND FRUIT

SAFETY WHEN EATING PLANTS AND FRUIT

Never eat or even taste a plant or a fruit you don't know; it could be poisonous!

Never eat mushrooms or fruits that smell like almonds.

Don't pick plants that grow in stagnant or dank water.

Finally, you should never pull up a plant you can't identify. It isn't ecological to do so because you might be destroying animal habitat.

The most important rule of all: as soon as you can, **ask a grownup for advice.**

42

❱ Recognize edible plants easily

◆ Coconut

Have you already eaten this fruit? It's delicious. Coconuts ripen at the top of coconut palms and then fall onto the beach when it's windy. Coconuts are very nutritious, and inside the fruit you'll find two cups of drinking water. But be careful: if you eat only coconuts, your intestines will suffer!

A little history

If our food stores are full of many edible fruits and vegetables, we can thank the great adventurers who discovered new continents despite the risk of their ships sinking at sea or being washed up on a desert island. Potatoes, sweet corn, tomatoes, kiwis, bananas, and pineapples are a small example of the foods these adventurers brought back from their voyages!

◆ Banana tree

Everything in a banana tree is good. Not only can you eat the fruit (even if the fruit on wild trees is smaller and not very sweet), you can eat the entire plant! You can eat bananas raw or cooked or fried. The plant and the flowers should be cut into small pieces and boiled in water.

◆ Manioc

Manioc is well known as typical castaway food. But strangely, it is rather hard to find growing naturally. If you find any on your island, pull it out of the ground and use the tubers, just like a potato. Peel them and cook them: never eat raw manioc.

◆ Bamboo shoots

Search around the base of adult bamboo: the young shoots look like pointed hats. When you snap them in two you'll see that they are juicy. Skin them and cut them into small slices before cooking them for a long time in boiling water.

◆ Papaya (pawpaw)

This plant is funny with its thick trunk and the fruits hanging from it! When they are green you can eat them as a vegetable; once they are orange, eat them as fruit.

◆ Seaweed

Some seaweed is edible, easy to find, and makes a great salad! The best seaweed is found attached to rocks. Ask a grownup for advice to make sure you don't mistake the type of seaweed before eating it. You can make delicious salads or dry it out to make flour and cook it in boiling water.

45

SAFETY FIRST!

✗ You can survive quite a long time without eating (a week or two depending on your height and weight). But be careful: if you don't eat anything for several days, your body will get weak! However, sometimes it's better not to eat anything than to eat something you're not sure about! The golden rule is that you only eat what is absolutely certain to be edible.

✗ If you only have a small store of food, don't waste anything, and ration yourself. Remember that it is important to drink properly before eating properly.

SIGNAL YOUR PRESENCE

HOW TO LET PEOPLE KNOW YOU ARE THERE

Even if you have everything you need on your desert island (you have found food, you have drinking water and a good shelter), you miss your family and friends. It's normal to have the blues and want to go home to the people you love.

That's why you should make sure that luck is on your side when a ship or a plane passes near or over your island.

But how do you attract their attention? How do you make yourself visible and make them understand that you are a castaway?

A little history

For centuries, sailors were on the lookout for the lights coming from lighthouses that signaled capes, dangerous areas, and ports where they could anchor. Aboard large ships a person (the Lookout) was chosen to climb to the top of the mast to spot the lights and tell the captain the route to follow. Today, lighthouses are beginning to disappear, replaced by geolocation instruments.

STEP 1

❱ Make distress signs that can be seen from a plane

Planes fly very high, so you'll need to make signs that are simple and very large, using scavenged materials such as logs, stones, or seaweed. Choose an open area, such as a clearing or the beach, which is the best place to set up your signs.

- **"Y"**

This is the international distress sign that all rescuers know. It's easy to make with long logs.

- **The famous "SOS"**

Everyone knows these three letters; they are an English acronym for Save Our Ship. This sign is a bit more complicated to make but is still very efficient.

- **"Three fires"**

The idea is to make a geometrical pattern that can be seen from the sky. If you build three fires in a perfect triangle, they will catch the eye of pilots flying over your island (see page 50).

With one of these signs, everything that flies over your island will know you are there—even the seagulls!

STEP 2

❭ Being seen from a ship passing a long way away

Now that your signals for being seen from the sky are in place on the beach, if you want to increase your chances of being seen, climb to the highest point on your island to make sure you can be seen from the farthest point on the horizon. As the Earth is round, you'll be seen more easily if you are high up than if you are on the beach!

• Fire
Light a fire on a rock, for example, so that distant ships can see it.

• Reflecting the sun
This can be done using objects such as a mirror, old CD, soda can, or metal spoon. First practice doing an "SOS": three rapid flashes, three long flashes, and three rapid flashes. Then use your fingers to fix on your target. This signal can be seen from miles away due to the force of the sun's reflection!

A little more history

To signal their shipwreck, some survivors wrote a distress message that they put in a bottle and threw into the sea, hoping someone would find it. But very few were rescued, because a bottle takes too long to wash ashore and be discovered! Bottles have been found after they have floated in the sea for over a hundred years. This method really isn't fast enough!

• A wheel of light

This is done at night using a torch. With the torch in your hand, hold your arm out in front of you and turn it fast in a circular movement. This will create a "wheel" of light that will attract the attention of passing ships.

THAT LITTLE EXTRA

Every ship carries a survival kit that usually contains a foghorn or whistle that you can use to signal your presence—if you are lucky enough to find it.

DID YOU KNOW?

Most distress signals are sent by radio. If you have the chance to use one, and only if you are truly in great difficulty, turn to the emergency band—channel 16—and shout, "Mayday, Mayday!" Everyone will understand that you are in danger somewhere. If someone answers, remain calm and answer all the questions you are asked.

SAFETY FIRST!

✗ Never light a fire without a grownup being nearby.
✗ If you aren't in a real survival situation, don't forget to take your distress signs apart to avoid launching search parties for nothing.
✗ When lifting heavy rocks to form your signs, be careful not to drop one on your toes.

READ THE SKY

STARS AND CLOUDS

It's really nice to lie back on the sand at night and look up at the sky!

But apart from dreaming and watching shooting stars, knowing how to "read the stars" is a really important part of survival. In the past, the great adventurers used the position of the stars to go from one continent to another and to sail the oceans without getting lost.

Even during the day you can find a lot of indications to guide you, thanks to the sun, and predict the weather with the clouds.

❯ Understanding the sun's movements

This is an excellent method for finding your direction! Every day, the sun rises in the east. At midday, it is at its highest point and is in the south. In the evening it sinks in the west. This will help you mark out the four cardinal points.

DID YOU KNOW?

In the summer, when you look at the night sky, you must have noticed that there is a long, whitish band made up of trillions of stars. This zone is called the Milky Way, due to its milky color.

East

South

North

West

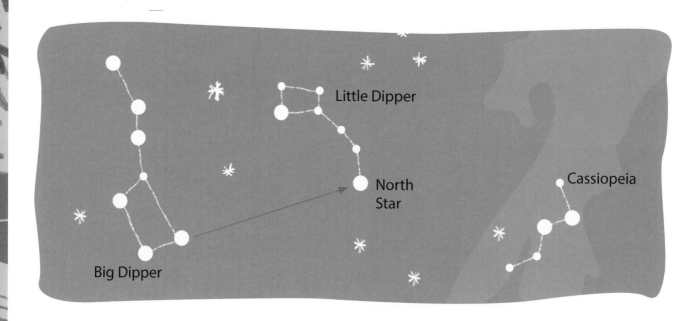

Little Dipper

North Star

Cassiopeia

Big Dipper

❭ Using the stars to find north

Of course, you can only see the stars at night! And if there is only one star you should know to chart your direction, it's the North Star (the Pole Star)! This is a small star, a little isolated, and no brighter than the others. The thing that makes it special is that it remains fixed in the sky while the other stars turn round it, as if it was the center of a spinning top! If you can find it, you will have found the direction for heading north.

• The Big Dipper

It's the third-largest constellation and the first we learn to find in the sky. You'll see that it's easy to recognize; it's part of the Ursa Major constellation, that always turns round the North Star. It will take you directly to the North Star!

• The Little Dipper

Once you have found the North Star, it's easy to find the Little Dipper, sometimes called the Little Bear.

• Cassiopeia

This group of stars is easy to find. Cassiopeia has the shape of a "W," a bit squashed on the left, or a backward "3." You'll find it opposite the Big Dipper. This small constellation revoles round the Pole Star. It's said that Cassiopeia always looks toward the north!

❯ Other remarkable constellations

• The constellation of Orion
Everyone has seen this huge constellation. Search the sky to find seven stars in the shape of a bowtie or hourglass. You have found the body of the legendary hunter, Orion. With the help of a grownup you will find his legs, arms, son, dagger, and bow.

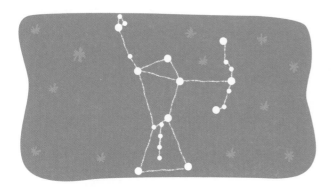

• The constellation of the Swan
This is a constellation made up of beautiful bright stars. You have to imagine a bird in full flight, its wings spread out, and its neck long and graceful. It spreads out along the Milky Way toward the south.

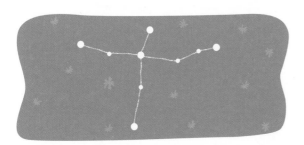

❯ Recognize different clouds to predict the weather

• Big black clouds: nimbostratus, cumulonimbus, or cumulus
Normally, these aren't signs of good weather! If the wind blows them in your direction, don't be surprised if you are caught up in a heavy shower.

• Wispy white clouds: cirrus
Not many people know that these clouds are made up of ice crystals. But they are so high in the sky that they don't bring rain. On the other hand, they cover the sky like a veil, stopping you from using the sun to light your fire.

DID YOU KNOW?

A shooting star is really a small stone about the size of a marble. When it enters Earth's atmosphere, the friction caused by the air against the stone gets so hot that it bursts into flame, which is the light we see, until it burns out. Every night there are about seven meteoroids (shooting starts) per hour that enter the Earth's atmosphere, but very few of them reach the ground.

PREVENTION AND TREATMENT

PROTECTING YOURSELF AND
APPLYING FIRST AID

❭ Protect your skin from the sun

On your desert island, the sun is going to be your main enemy! But you'll easily find a shady spot to avoid overheating. Wearing a hat and sun block and drinking lots of water will prevent you from having hallucinations, fever, shivers, and sunburn. If you do get sunburn, you can quickly treat it by rubbing your skin with the juice from an aloe-vera plant. This plant can often be found growing along the edge of the beach.

❭ Scrapes and cuts

The slightest graze will take time to heal, because water, salt, and sand slow the healing process. If you don't have a first-aid kit, the best thing to do is to wash your wound in clean water and leave it to heal on its own. It will crust over, the scab will eventually fall off, and you'll be better. Now, if you want it to heal faster, look for a nice, thick spider web and lay it over your cut. It will heal much faster!

DID YOU KNOW?

To avoid getting bitten by a snake, you should follow certain safety measures. First, don't walk around barefoot; wear sturdy lace-up shoes, especially when walking through tall grass. When walking, clap your hands or stamp every few steps to frighten snakes away. Never put your hand into a pile of leaves or under rocks, in case a reptile is having a snooze there.

THAT LITTLE EXTRA

- Copy animals that lick their wounds. If you don't have anything handy to clean a scrape or cut, put your saliva on it. According to recent US studies, it contains healing agents.

- If you have a nose bleed, it sometimes helps to put a piece of paper under your tongue. It's strange—no one knows why, but it works.

❭ Insect and jellyfish stings

To ease the pain from a wasp, hornet, or jellyfish sting, put hot sand directly on the sting.

❭ Blisters on your feet

It's very important to check your feet every evening, especially if you have walked a lot during the day in lace-up shoes. If you have a blister, don't pop it. Clean it with clear water and leave your foot bare. If you have to keep walking, put a plantain or banana leaf between your sock and the blister. These leaves will protect your blister and keep the blister from getting worse.

SAFETY FIRST!

✗ Don't stay too long in the sun without sun block and a hat.

✗ Don't walk barefoot anywhere except on the sand. On rocks, in the grass, or the forest, wear sturdy shoes.

✗ Be careful when using sharp instruments (ask for advice from a grownup if necessary).

Originally published as *Manuel de Survie sur une Ile Déserte* by Vagnon. ©Vagnon 2017
Translated from the French by Omicron Language Solutions, LLC.

Library of Congress Control Number: 2018958792

Type set in Woodstamp/HVD Peace/HVD Poster/GelDoticaJumpyHeavy/Myriad Pro

ISBN: 978-0-7643-5706-0
Printed in China

Published by Schiffer Publishing, Ltd.
4880 Lower Valley Road
Atglen, PA 19310
Phone: (610) 593-1777; Fax: (610) 593-2002
E-mail: Info@schifferbooks.com
Web: www.schifferbooks.com

For our complete selection of fine books on this and related subjects, please visit our website at www.schifferbooks.com. You may also write for a free catalog.

Schiffer Publishing's titles are available at special discounts for bulk purchases for sales promotions or premiums. Special editions, including personalized covers, corporate imprints, and excerpts, can be created in large quantities for special needs. For more information, contact the publisher.

We are always looking for people to write books on new and related subjects. If you have an idea for a book, please contact us at proposals@schifferbooks.com.